PDP Cornell Notes

PDP Cornell Notes

A Systematic Strategy
to
Aid Comprehension

by

Julie Adams, MAT, NBCT
of
Adams Educational Consulting

Prepare the child for the path, not the path for the child.

iUniverse, Inc.
New York   Bloomington

PDP Cornell Notes
A Systematic Strategy to Aid Comprehension

iUniverse books may be ordered through booksellers or by contacting:

iUniverse
1663 Liberty Drive
Bloomington, IN 47403
www.iuniverse.com
1-800-Authors (1-800-288-4677)

ISBN: 978-1-4502-4593-7 (pbk)
ISBN: 978-1-4502-4594-4 (ebk)

Ann Olmos-Arreola—Spanish translations

Debbie Markham, All Phase Photography—Author Photo

Printed in the United States of America

iUniverse rev. date: 9/7/10

Dear Educator,

Welcome to <u>PDP CORNELL NOTES</u>. I hope you find this book to be a valuable tool in teaching your students my systematic note-taking strategy dubbed ***PDP Cornell Notes***, **PDP stands for Pre-During-Post**. This powerful strategy and workbook are a result of my own experience working with adolescents who often struggle with understanding their non-fiction readings and organizing their thoughts and facts during the reading process. After experimenting with many note-taking strategies but not liking any of them in their entirety, I pulled ideas from several and developed this comprehensive Pre-During-Post method and experienced tremendous success.

When learning a strategy such as this, it is less 'painful' for the students if the text is reader friendly and high interest; therefore, the article topics included were chosen by my own students and are short and engaging. After students have mastered the strategy using the adolescent friendly articles in this workbook, transition them in to using it with complex textbook readings.

Included are "scaffolded" note-taking structures for each article in which the study questions and vocabulary terms are already identified, expediting the frontloading process. However, you may find the blank *PDP Cornell Notes* form to be more useful so students can develop their own study questions based on the sub-headings or they can use binder paper and bypass the note-taking forms all together.

For best retention, encourage students to immediately study their notes for three minutes, three or four times, over a forty-eight hour period.

**Note-I am not a doctor so the suggestions in the articles are merely that, helpful tips from my own experience.

Happy PDP Cornell Note-taking!

The Steps to PDP Cornell Notes

FRONTLOADING

1. Pre-read and write prediction statement

2. Identify and define vocabulary

3. Form *who, what, when, where, why, how* study questions based on sub-headings

DURING READING

4. Read to answer study questions

POST READING

5. Write a *"Paragraph Shrink"* statement to summarize the text (one complete sentence, 20 words or less), using the *"Focus Words"*

How to Pre-Read an Article

1. Read the title and subtitle

2. Read the subheadings within the article

3. Analyze any visual aids (graphs, maps, pictures), this is known as *functional analysis*

4. Identify typographical aids (**bold**, *italicized*, or *underlined* words) and define them

5. Scan end of text material (review questions, summary, footnotes, etc.), if provided

6. Write a prediction statement on the ***PDP Cornell Notes*** form

Name_____Title of Text_____

Prediction_____

PreDuringPostCornell Notes

<u>Questions</u>

<u>Answers</u>

<u>Vocabulary</u>

<u>Paragraph Shrink</u>
Focus Words:

PDP Cornell Notes
Peer-Editing Form

Name _____   Peer Editor _____

Title of Notes _____

1. Is there a prediction statement? Yes   No

2. Are the study questions numbered? Yes   No

3. Is there adequate spacing between each study question or are they crammed together? Adequate spacing? Yes   No

4. Are the answers to the questions numbered? Yes   No

5. Is there an answer for each study question? Yes   No
If not, which one/s is/are missing an answer?

_____

6. Is the vocabulary defined in the vocabulary section? Yes   No

7. Is the paragraph "shrink" statement one *complete* sentence, 20 words or less? Yes   No

If not, what needs to be fixed? _____

8. Are the "focus" words used in the paragraph "shrink" statement? Yes   No

9. Are the notes written in a neat and organized manner? Yes   No

10. Suggestions for improvement:

J. Adams/AEC/2010

Index of Articles

Adolescent Sleep
Julia Adams

1) You used to wake up early every morning, energetic for the day's adventures. What happened? Why can't you fall asleep early and wake up refreshed for your first period class? These might be questions you ask yourself as you progress through adolescence (ages 11-20). But don't fret, you are not alone.

Puberty Changes Sleep Patterns

2) As children grow older and enter puberty, their brains and bodies change and they often develop different sleep patterns. Our brains produce a hormone called *melatonin*, a hormone that helps a person feel relaxed and sleepy.

3) An adolescent brain often produces melatonin later in the day than a younger child or adult's brain, making it difficult to fall asleep early and wake up early. Therefore, a teen sometimes is not sleepy until 10 or 11 o'clock at night.

Adolescent Sleep Needs & Health

4) The recommended amount of sleep for adolescents is 9 hours. However, not falling asleep until very late makes it difficult to receive enough sleep. Inadequate sleep can negatively *affect* one's health. The *effects* of sleep *deprivation* are: fatigue (of course), irritability, and the inability to concentrate, problem solve and/or remember information.

A lack of sleep can even lead to a lack of self-confidence, which can develop into *depression*, or feeling very unhappy for a long period. Adolescents sometimes struggle in these areas.

Suggestions for Better Sleep

5) How can adolescents acquire better sleep? Stop drinking caffeinated beverages after 3pm or all together, exercise regularly for 45-60 minutes but not within 3 hours of sleep, and turn off electronics (TV, computer, etc.) 60 minutes prior to going to bed. In addition, dimming the lights, listening to relaxing music or reading something enjoyable can help send you to dreamland.

El Sueño del Adolescente
Julie Adams

1) Te levantabas temprano cada mañana, energético para las aventuras del día. ¿Qué sucedió? ¿Por qué no te puedes dormir temprano y despertarte refrescado para tu primer periodo de clases? Estas pudieran ser preguntas que te hagas a ti mismo al pasar por la adolescencia (edades del 11-20). Pero no te preocupes, no estás solo.

La Pubertad Cambia los Patrones del Sueño
2) Al crecer de edad y entrar en la pubertad, los cerebros y cuerpos de los niños cambian y a menudo desarrollan diferentes patrones de sueño. Nuestros cerebros producen una hormona llamada *melatonina*, una hormona que ayuda a que una persona se sienta relajada y somnolienta.

3) El cerebro de un adolescente a menudo produce melatonina más tarde en el día que el cerebro de un niño más joven o de un adulto, haciéndolo más dificultoso para dormirse temprano y despertar temprano. Por lo tanto, un adolescente a veces no está somnoliento hasta las 10 u 11 de la noche.

Necesidades y Salud del Sueño de un Adolescente
4) La cantidad recomendada de sueño para adolescentes es 9 horas. Sin embargo, no dormirse hasta muy tarde hace dificultoso el tener suficientes horas para hormir. Sueño inadecuado puede *afectar* negativamente neustra salud. Los *efectos* de la *depravación* de sueño son: fatiga (desde luego), irritabilidad, y la inhabilidad de concentración, solución de problemas y/o recuerdo de información. Falta de sueño inclusive puede llevar a falta de confianza en sí mismo, lo cual se puede desarrollar en *depresión*, o sentirse muy infeliz por mucho tiempo. Los adolescentes a menudo batallan en estas áreas.

Sugerencias para un Mejor Sueño
5) ¿Cómo pueden los adolescentes obtener un mejor sueño? Deja de beber totalmente bebidas con cafeína después de las 3 de la tarde, ejercita regularmente durante 45-60 minutos pero no dentro de 3 horas de dormir, y apaga los electrónicos (TV, computadora, etc.) 60 minutos antes de acostrate. Adicionalmente, bajando las luces, escuchando a música relajante o leyendo algo agradable te puede mandar al mundo de ensueños.

Name_____ Title of Text: "Adolescent Sleep"

Prediction: I predict this article is about...

PreDuringPostCornell Notes

Questions	Answers

1. **How** does puberty change sleep patterns?

1.

2. **What** are adolescent sleep needs and **how** does it affect my health?

2.

3. **What** are some suggestions for better sleep?

3.

Vocabulary	Paragraph Shrink **Focus Words:**

melatonin-

affect-

effect-

deprivation-

depression-

J.Adams/AEC/2010

The 5 Second Rule
Julie Adams

1) Nearly everyone has dropped food on the floor and been tempted to eat it based on the "5 Second Rule," but what does science really say about it?

What is the 5 Second Rule?

2) The 5 Second Rule is an old wives' tale that states food dropped on the floor is safe and clean enough to eat as long as it is picked up within 5 seconds. And people all over have used this "rule" to justify the gummy bear or piece of bologna they eat after dropping it on the floor.

Is this "Rule" True or False?

3) Jillian Clarke, a high school student who was interning at the University of Illinois, tested the 5 Second Rule. After dropping gummy bears and cookies on various floors throughout the university, she discovered that some floors contained only small amounts of bacteria, which may be safe to eat from. *Bacteria* are small living things that can cause illness, and often can only be seen through a microscope.

4) However, most floors were so bacteria filled, the food that touched the surface of those floors was instantly *contaminated* and unsafe for *consumption*. It didn't even take 5 seconds.

Some Foods Riskier Than Others

5) Research has shown that drier foods such as crackers, are less likely to pick up bacteria as it is more difficult for the bacteria to *adhere*, or stick, to them. Moist foods like meat and cheese absorb bacteria quicker and deeper so even wiping them off before eating, does not make it safe.

Don't Judge a Floor by its Looks

6) Some floors look shiny and clean enough to eat from but don't be fooled. Floors are only as clean as the object that cleaned them. Would you want to eat something found in that mop used in the cafeteria? Yuck, of course not.

7) What about carpet? It seems cleaner and more sanitary doesn't it? Studies show that carpet can hide as much as 10 times its own weight in dirt and the average family tracks roughly three pounds of dirt into their homes each week.

When in Doubt, Throw it Out

8) If you are enjoying your favorite chocolate chip cookie and it slips through your fingers and crashes to the floor, the best thing to do is throw it away and get another cookie. Consuming bacteria can cause tummy troubles that you do not want to have.

La Regla de 5 Segundos
Julie Adams

1) Casi a todos se les ha caído comida al suelo y han tenido tentación de comérsela basado en la "Regla de 5 Segundos," pero, ¿que es lo que dice la ciencia realmente sobre esto?

¿Que es la Regla de 5 Segundos?

2) La Regla de 5 Segundos es un cuento de viejas que dice que la comida que se cae al suelo está suficientemente apta y limpia para consumo mientras se recoja dentro de 5 segundos. Y la gente por dondequiera ha usado esta "regla" para justificar el osito de gomita o pedazo de bolonia que se comen después de que se cayó al suelo.

¿Esta "Regla" es Verdadera o Falsa?

3) Jillian Clarke, una estudiante de la escuela secundaria quien ejercía como profesora en práctica en la Universidad de Illinois, puso a prueba la Regla de 5 Segundos. Después de tirar ositos de gomita y galletas en varios pisos de la universidad, descubrió que algunos pisos contenían solamente pequeñas cantidades de bacteria, la cual pudiera estar apta para consumo. Las *Bacterias* son pequeños organismos vivientes que pueden causar enfermedad, y que a menudo se pueden ver solamente por medio de un microscopio.

4) Sin embargo, la mayoría de los pisos estaban tan llenos de bacteria, que la comida que tocó la superficie de esos suelos se *contaminó* instantáneamente y no fue apta para *consumo*. Ni siquiera tomó 5 segundos

Algunas Comidas tienen más Riesgos que Otras

5) La investigación ha demonstrado que las comidas más secas tales como las galletas, son menos probables de contaminarse con bacteria ya que es más dificil para la bacteria adherirse, o pegarse a ellas. Las comidas húmedas tales como la carne y el queso absorben la bacteria en forma más rápida y penetrante por lo que aún limpiándolas antes de comer, no las hace aptas para el consumo.

No Juzgues a un Suelo por su Aspecto

6) Algunos pisos se ven suficientemente brillantes y limpios como para comer de ellos, pero no te engañes. Los pisos están solamente tan limpios como el objeto que los limpió. ¿Te gustaría comer algo del trapeador usado en la cafetería? ¡Puaj, claro que no!

7) ¿Qué tal la alfombra? ¿Parece más limpia y más sanitaria, verdad? Los estudios demuestran que la alfombra puede esconder tanto como 10 veces su propio peso en mugre y que la familia típica trae tres libras de mugre a casa cada semana.

Cuando en Duda, Tíralo

8) Si estás gozando tu galleta favorita con trocitos de chocolate y se te cae al suelo, lo mejor que puedes hacer es tirarla y tomar otra galleta. Consumiendo bacteria puede causarte problemas estomacales que no tienes que tener.

Name_____ Title of Text: "The 5 Second Rule"

Prediction: I predict this article is about...

PreDuringPostCornell Notes

Questions	Answers
1. **What** is the 5 Second Rule?	1.
2. **Is** this rule true or false?	2.
3. **Are** some foods riskier than others?	3.
4. **Is** a floor clean if it looks clean?	4.
5. **If** I am not sure, what should I do?	5.

Vocabulary	Paragraph Shrink Focus Words:
bacteria-	
contaminated-	
consumption-	
adhere-	

Are Kids too Connected?
Julie Adams

1) You spend all day in school and you can't wait to get home to relax and enjoy some time on your computer. You hop on to play a video game or two or to check out your social networking site of choice, only to look at the clock and realize hours have gone by and you haven't even completed your homework yet. Now you are frustrated and depressed, but not because you have homework to do, you are upset because you have to get off the computer. Sound familiar? You may be developing what experts are now calling Internet or Gaming *Addiction*.

What is it?

2) Internet or Gaming Addiction is when one becomes so hooked on being "connected" to the computer that when you are not on the computer, you feel grumpy, tired or anxious. And the only time you feel happy is when you are playing that game or chatting on your online social network. Some *symptoms* of internet addiction are: most non-school hours are spent on the computer, falling asleep in school, falling behind on school assignments and lower grades, lying about computer use or choosing to be on the computer instead of interacting face-to-face with people.

Physical Problems with Computer Addiction

3) Many health professionals are seeing problems associated with too much computer use. These problems may be the development of Carpal Tunnel Syndrome, sleep disturbances, back or neck aches, headaches, or eye-strain.

Is it dangerous?

4) Experts say this phenomenon may lead to dangerous *consequences*. Online gaming allows shy people to be more aggressive, and those who feel powerless over their lives to have a sense of control. This alone is not a problem but when coupled with feelings of isolation often resulting from too much computer use and the stress of our daily lives, this can lead to serious social and emotional problems.

5) Social networking sites and chat rooms allow one to be more bold and say and post things one wouldn't normally say, which can lead to negative consequences as well.

Recommendations

6) Experts urge adolescent computer use be limited to no more than 1 hour per day. Exercise and being involved with sports, clubs or charity work can also prevent online addiction.

¿Están muy Conectados los Niños?
Julie Adams

1) Pasas todo el día en la escuela y estás impaciente para llegar a casa para relajarte y gozar un rato en tu computadora. Brincas para jugar uno o dos juegos de video o para revisar el sitio de tu red social de tu elección, solo para ver al reloj y realizar que han pasado las horas y que tú no has terminado todavía tu tarea. Ahora estás frustrado y deprimido, pero no porque tienes tarea que hacer; estás disgustado porque tienes que dejar la computadora. ¿Suena familiar? Pudieras estar desarrollando lo que los expertos están nombrando ahora *Adicción* al Internet o a la Jugada.

¿Qué es Eso?
2) Adicción al Internet o a la Jugada es cuando uno se envicia tanto en estar "conectado" a la computadora que cuando no estás en la computadora, te sientes malhumorado, cansado o ansioso. Y el único tiempo cuando te sientes contento es cuando estás jugando ese juego o chateando en tu red social en linea. Algunos *síntomas* de adicción al internet son: la mayoría de las horas fuera de la escuela son gastadas en la computadora, durmiendo en la escuela, retrasándote en tus tareas escolares y calificaciones bajas, mintiendo sobre el uso de la computadora o eligiendo a estar en la computadora en lugar de relacionarse cara a cara con la gente.

Problemas Físicos con la Adicción a la Computadora
3) Muchos profesionales de la salud están viendo problemas asociados con mlucho uso de la computadora. Estos problemas pueden causar el desarrollo del Síndrome del Túnel Carpiano, disturbios del sueño, dolores de la espalda o del cuello, jaquecas, o vista cansada.

¿Es Peligroso?
4) Los expertos dicen que este fenómeno puede llevar a *consecuencias* peligrosas. La jugada en línea permite a la gente cohibida a ser más agresiva, y a aquellos que se sienten impotentes sobre sus vidas a tener un sentido de control. Esto solo no es un problems pero cuando es acoplado con sentimientos de aislamiento a menudo resultando en demasiado use de computadora y la tensión de nuestras vidas cotidianas, esto puede llevar a problemas sociales y emocionales serios.

5) Sitios de redes sociales y salas de charla permiten a que uno sea más descarado y decir y poner cosas que uno no diría normalmente, lo cual puede llevar también a consecuencias negativas.

Recomendaciones
6) Los expertos urgen a que el uso de computadoras por adolescentes sea limitado a no más de 1 hora al día. El ejercicio y el involucrarse en deportes, clubs o trabalo comunitario también puede prevenir la adicción en línea.

Name_____ Title of Text: "Are Kids Too Connected?"

Prediction: I predict this article is about...

PreDuringPostCornell Notes

Questions	Answers
1. **What** is Internet or Gaming Addiction?	1.
2. **What** are physical problems associated with this addiction?	2.
3. **Is** it dangerous?	3.
4. **What** are the recommendations to avoid this addiction?	4.

Vocabulary

Paragraph Shrink
Focus Words:

addiction-

symptom-

consequence-

J.Adams/AEC/2010

The Most Important Meal
Julie Adams

1) Studies show that students who eat breakfast do better in school. In fact, eating breakfast can make you more successful in just about everything you do.

Why is Breakfast Important?

2) Breakfast is important because it does just as it says (break/fast). Eating breakfast breaks the *fast* endured while you slept. It is even more important for children and adolescents to eat breakfast because their growing bodies and developing brains rely on the regular intake of food to thrive. When people skip breakfast, they may go as long as 18 hours without food. This semi-starvation can create many physical, emotional and behavioral problems for them.

A Healthy Start

3) A healthy breakfast should contain some protein and fiber. Protein can come from meat, eggs, dairy or beans. Fiber can be found in whole grains, vegetables and fruits. A good example of a healthy breakfast may be something like two eggs, a piece of whole grain toast, an apple and a glass of milk. This meal supplies the nutrients the body needs for energy and concentration. And a balanced meal like this satisfies your hunger.

The Sugar Cycle

4) Stay away from sugary cereals, syrups and pastries because they are loaded with sugar and are digested too quickly. This leaves you feeling hungry and tired in a few hours.

Break the Fast to Lose Weight

5) Some people skip breakfast to lose weight. However, studies have shown that the opposite occurs. When people go several hours without eating, the body clings to all of its *resources*, including fat, so skipping breakfast does not help one lose weight, it can actually cause you to gain weight. In fact, people who eat a healthy breakfast are more likely to lose weight as they tend to make healthier choices through the day.

Better Choices = Better Results

6) So if you want to feel energized and prepared to take on your busy schedule and maintain a healthy weight at the same time, eat a balanced breakfast to give your body what it needs to succeed.

La Comida más Importante
Julie Adams

1) Los estudios han demonstrado que los estudiantes que se desayunan les va mejor en la escuela. Por hecho, desayunándote te puede hacer más exitoso en casi todo lo que haces.

¿Por qué es el Desayuno Importante?

2) El desayuno es importante porque hace exactamente lo que dice (quitar/ayuno). Desayunándote rompe el *ayuno* perdurado mientras dormías. Es aún más importante que los niños y los adolescentes se desayunen porque sus cuerpos crecientes y sus cerebros en desarrollo dependen en el consumo regular de comida para crecer confuerzas. Cuando la gente no se desayuna, pueden pasar tantas como 18 horas sin comida. Esta semihambre puede crear para ellas muchos problemas físicos, emocionales y de comportamiento.

Un Comienzo Saludable

3) Un desayuno saludable debe de contener algunas proteínas y fibra. La proteína puede venir de la carne, huevos, productos lácteos o frijoles. La fibra puede encontrarse en cereales integrales, vegetales y frutas. Un buen ejemplo de un desayuno saludable pudiera ser algo como un par de huevos, un pedazo de pan integral tostado, una manzana y un vaso de leche. Esta comida suple los nutrientes que el cuerpo necesita para energía y concentración, y una comida balanceada como esta satisface tu hambre.

El Ciclo del Azúcar

4) Aléjate de los cereales azucarados, mieles y pastelillos debido a que están cargados con azúcar y se digieren muy rápido. Esto te deja sintiéndote con hambre ya cansado en unas cuantas horas.

Rompe el Ayuno para Perder Peso

5) Alguna gente omite el desayuno para perder peso. Sin embargo, los estudios han demostrado que lo opuesto es lo que sucede. Cuando la gente pasa varias horas sin comer, el cuerpo se apega a todos sus *recursos*, incluyendo grasa, por lo que omitiendo el desayuno no ayuda a que uno pierda peso; realmente puede causarte que aumentes de peso. En realidad, la gente que come un desayuno saludable es más fácil que pierda peso ya que tienden a hacer elecciones más saludables durante el día.

Mejores Elecciones=Mejores Resultados

6) Por lo tanto, si quieres sentirte con energía y preparado para enfrentarte a tu horario ocupado y mantener un peso saludable a la misma vez, come un desayuno balanceado para darle a tu cuerpo lo que necesita para tener éxito.

Name_____ Title of Text: "The Most Important Meal"

Prediction: I predict this article is about...

PreDuringPostCornell Notes

<u>Questions</u>

<u>Answers</u>

1. **Why** is breakfast so important?

1.

2. **What** does a healthy breakfast include?

2.

3. **Why** are sugary choices not the best choices?

3.

4. **Why** do I need to break the fast to lose weight?

4.

5. **How** can I feel energized and maintain a healthy weight?

5.

<u>Vocabulary</u>

<u>Paragraph Shrink</u>
Focus Words:

fast-

resources-

J.Adams/AEC/2010

Talking to Your Parents
Julie Adams

1) As an adolescent, there will be times when you really need to talk to and hear from your parents or a trusted adult. You may feel a bit uncomfortable talking about a difficult topic, but understanding how to establish a solid line of communication will allow you to *communicate* more effectively with the adults in your life.

Establishing a Foundation

2) Sometimes it may seem that most of the discussions with your parents end in frustration or arguments. However, a positive line of communication can be established by following these principles. First, chat with your parent every day about small things that happen such as what funny thing your teacher said or a new trick your pet has learned. Also, ask your parent about his day or what he hopes to do on the weekend. Talking everyday about trivial things can lay the *foundation* for a trusting relationship where deeper feelings and situations can be discussed. Asking your parent questions about his life shows that you care and want to know more about him as a person. Next, thank your parent for the help he has provided or what he has bought for you to let him know you truly appreciate his time, energy and money.

A Good Time

3) Ask them when would be a good time to discuss something important. Trying to discuss a serious topic while they are watching the news or rushing to finish a project is not ideal. Dinner or bedtime is often a relaxed and calm environment for serious conversations.

Identify Your Needs

4) Decide first what you need from them. Do you need advice, someone to listen or permission to do something? Let them know in the beginning, "I have a problem and I just want you to listen so you know what is bothering me, I don't want any advice right now." Stating your needs like this helps to clarify the role you want them to play: a listener, a problem solver or a permission granter.

Identify Your Feelings

5) It's natural to feel nervous about a serious topic but don't let your emotions ruin an opportunity for discussion. Put your feelings into words to start the conversation, "Mom, I need to talk to you about something really embarrassing." Letting her know your feelings on the subject will help her to understand the situation better.

Mind Your Manners

6) Always be respectful, calm and make eye contact when speaking to your parents as this is the best way to communicate effectively with anyone.

Hablando con tus Padres
Julie Adams

1) Como adolescente, habrán veces cuando tú realmente necesitas hablar y escuchar de tus padres o de un adulto confiable. Pudieras sentirte un poco inconfortable hablando sobre un tópico dificultoso, pero entendiendo como establecer una línea sólida de communicación te permitirá *communicarte* más efectivamente con los adultos en tu vida.

Estableciendo una Base

2) A veces parecería que la mayoría de las discusiones con tus padres terminan en frustraciones o discusiones. Sin embargo, una línea positiva de communicadión puede establescerse siguiendo estos principios. Primero, charla con tus padres cada día sobre pequeñeces que suceden tales como las cosas chistosas que dijo tu profesor o un truco neuvo que aprendió tu mascota. También, pregúntales a tus padres sobre su día o lo que piensa hacer el fin de semana. Hablando diariamente sobre cosas triviales puede establecer la *fundación* para una relación de confianza donde los sentimientos más profundos y situaciones pueden ser discutidos. Haciendo preguntas a tu padre sobre su vida demuestra que te importa y que quieres saber más sobre él como persona. Enseguida, dale las gracias a tu padre por la ayuda que te ha brindado o por lo que te ha comprado para hacerle saber que tú verdaderamente aprecias su tiempo, energía y dinero.

Un Buen Tiempo

3) Pregúntales cuando sería un tiempo apto para discutir algo importante. Tratar de discutir un tópico serio mienteras ellos ven las noticias o apurando para terminar un proyecto no es ideal. Durante la cena o a la hora de acostarse es a menudo un ambiente relajado y calmado para conversaciones serias.

Identifica tus Necesidades

4) Decide primero que es lo que necesitas de ellos. ¿Necesitas consejo, alguien que te escuche o permiso para hacer algo? Déjales saber al principio, "Tengo un problema y nada más quiero que escuchen para que sepan lo que me está molestando; no quiero consejos ahora." Expresando tus necesidades en esta forma ayuda a clarificar el papel que tú quieres que ellos hagan: un oyente, solucionador de problema u otorgador de permiso.

Identifica Tus Sentimientos

5) Es natural sentirte nervioso sobre un tópico serio pero no dejes que tus emociones arruinen una oportunidad de discusión. Pon tus sentimientos en palabras para comenzar la discusión, "Mamá, necesito hablarte sobre algo que es verdaderamente embarazoso." Dejándole saber tus sentimientos sobre la materia la ayudará mejor entender la situación.

Cuida Tus Modales

6) Se siempre respetuoso, calmado y haz contacto visual al hablar con tus padres ya que esta es la mejor forma de communicarse efectivamente con quien sea.

Name_____ Title of Text: "Talking to Your Parents"

Prediction: I predict this article is about...

PreDuringPostCornell Notes

Questions	Answers

Questions

1. **How** can I establish a foundation for communication?

2. **When** is a good time to talk?

3. **Why** and **how** should I identify my needs?

4. **Why** should I identify my feelings?

5. **How** do I use my manners?

Vocabulary

communicate-

foundation-

Answers

1.

2.

3.

4.

5.

Paragraph Shrink
Focus Words:

Cyberbullying
Julie Adams

What is It?

1) If you are like most adolescents these days, you spend a lot of time on the computer and phone communicating with friends, downloading music and uploading photos. Chances are, you have been or will be a victim of cyberbullying at some point.

2) *Cyberbullying*, otherwise referred to as online or e-bullying, is when someone bullies another by sending messages over a computer or phone. It is classified as a *cybercrime*, which is a crime committed using a computer or the Internet, and you can be arrested.

Forms of Cyberbullying

3) A victim may be cyberbullied when private information or lies are spread on the internet about the person, private pictures are posted of someone without *consent*, or permission, or threatening and hateful messages are sent to cause harm.

Why Bully This Way?

4) When cyberbullies were asked why they bullied their victims in this way, most say because it was funny. They also said they were encouraged by their friends to do it, it was easier to do on a computer or phone because they didn't have to look the victim in the eye, they thought they wouldn't get caught or they didn't know it was illegal. Girls are twice as likely to engage in this form of bullying than boys. As is the case with all forms of bullying, the bully wants to feel powerful by making the victim feel helpless and humiliated.

Prevent Cyberbullying

5) To prevent cyberbullying, follow these suggestions. First, always keep the computer in a public area of the house so adults can *monitor* whom you are communicating with and be aware of any bullying that may happen. Second, keep personal information private—do not give your phone number, address, physical description, school or friends' names to any person on the internet.

6) Next, Stop-Print-Block-Tell. This means if you are a victim, stop communicating with the bully and save and print the message so you have a copy. Then, *establish* a block so no more messages can come through from the bully. Last, tell a trusted adult what happened so you are not alone in handling the situation.

7) Finally, TAKE 5. If anyone has angered you, take five minutes to calm down and think rationally before you respond to the person. Or you may find that no response is the best response. This will help you from becoming a cyberbully.

Ciberacoso
Julie Adams

¿Que es esto?

1) Si tú eres comom la mayoría de los adolescentes estos día, tú pasas mucho tiempo en la computadora y comunicándote con tus amistades, bajando música y subiendo fotos. Las probabilidades son, que tú has sido o serás una víctima de ciberacoso en algún momento.

2) *Ciberacoso*, de otra forma referido como acoso en línea o acoso electrónica, es cuando alguien acosa a otro mandando mensajes por computadora o por teléfono. Está clasificado como *cibedrcrímen*, el cual es un crimen cometido usando una computadora o el Internet, y puedes ser arrestado.

Formas de Ciberacoso

3) Una víctima puede ser ciberacosada cuando información privada o mentiras son difundidas en el internet sobre la persona, gráficas privadas son expuestas sin *consentimiento*, o permiso, o mensajes amenazadores y odiosos son mandados para causar daño.

¿Porqué Acosar en Esta Forma?

4) Cuando se les preguntó a los ciberacosadores porqué acosaban a sus víctimas en esta forma, la mayoría dijeron que era chistoso. También dijeron que fueron animados por sus amistades a hacerlo, que era más fácil hacerlo en una computadora o teléfono porque no tenian que ver a la víctima, ellos pensaron que no ser'*an* aprendidos o que no sabían que era ilegal. Las muchachas son más fácil de participar en esta forma de acoso que los muchachos. Como es el caso con todas formas de acoso, el acosador quiere sentirese más poderoso haciendo que la víctima se sienta indefensa y humillada.

Previene el Ciberacoso

5) Para prevenir el ciberacoso, sigue estas sugerencias. Primero, mantén siempre la computadora dentro de una área pública de la casa para que los adultos puedan *revisar* con quién te estás communicando y estar conscientes de cualquier acosamiento que pudiera suceder. Segundo, mantén la información personal privada—no des tu número telefónico, domicilio, descripción física, nombre de la escuela o de amistades a ninguna persona en el internet.

6) Seguidamente, Para-Copia-Bloque-Di. Esto quiere decir que si eres una víctima, para de comunicarte con el acosador y guarda y copia el mensaje para que tengas una copia. Entonces, *establece* un bloqueo para que ningún mensaje del acosador pueda recibirse. Finalmente, di a un adulto confiable lo que sucedió para que no estés solo tratando con la situación.

7) Finalmente, TOMA 5. Si alguien te ha hecho enojar, toma 5 minutos para calmarte y pensar racionalmente antes de responder a la persona. O pudieras encontrar que el no responder es la mejor respuesta. Esto te ayudará a no ser un ciberacosador.

Name_____ Title of Text: "Cyberbullying"

Prediction: I predict this article is about...

PreDuringPost Cornell Notes

Questions	Answers
<u>Questions</u>	<u>Answers</u>
1. **What** is it?	1.
2. **What** are the forms of cyberbullying?	2.
3. **Why** do people bully this way?	3.
4. **How** can I prevent this?	4.

<u>Vocabulary</u>

cyberbullying-

cybercrime-

consent-

monitor-

establish-

<u>Paragraph Shrink</u>
Focus Words:

J.Adams/AEC/2010

Test-Taking Tips
Julie Adams

1) Do you get butterflies in your stomach as soon as your teacher announces a test? Don't worry, you are not alone. *Test anxiety* is when a student worries excessively about taking a test. You may feel you are not *prepared*, you won't have enough time to finish, or if you don't do well on one test, you will fail the whole class. No matter what the reason, many people feel *overwhelmed* at the idea of taking a test.

Reduce Test-Taking Anxiety

2) There are many things one can do to reduce or even eliminate test anxiety. First, being well-prepared is the best way to reduce this feeling. Start studying and reviewing for your test days or even weeks ahead of time so you aren't trying to "cram" the night before. Next, exercising 45-60 minutes each day helps to reduce overall stress and can improve your concentration and memory. Other ways to reduce test stress are to get a good night's sleep, eat a healthy breakfast with protein, and show up to class early so you can look over your notes one last time. Following these suggestions will help you feel better prepared, but what can you do when you are taking the test?

Tips for Better Testing

3) Once you have the test in your hands you may think there is nothing left to do but worry. However, you can be a smarter test-taker by following these tips:

*Carefully read the directions 3 times so you know what you are expected to do. If you are confused about something, ask your teacher.

*Read the entire test so you know how much time you have to spend on each problem.

*Write down important formulas, definitions, or facts in the margins so you don't worry about forgetting them.

*Answer the easy problems first; this helps you feel more confident.

*Before marking your answer, read all of the choices and cross out the ones you know are not correct.

*If you feel nervous, slow down and take 3-4 deep breaths, this will help you focus.

*Finally, look over your answers and make sure you have answered every question.

4) Test-taking can be stressful, but being prepared and following these tips will help you to relax and do your best.

Consejos para Tomar Pruebas
Julie Adams

1) ¿Sientes mariposas en el estomago tan pronto como el profesor anuncia una prueba? No te preocupes, so estás solo. *Ansiedad de Prueba* es cuando un estudiante se preocupa excesivamente por tomar una prueba. Pudieras sentirte que no estás *preparado*, que no tendrás suficientemente tiempo para terminar, o que si no te va bien en la prueba, reprobarás toda la clase. No importa la razón, mucha gente se siente *abrumada* por la idea de tomar una prueba.

Reduce la Ansiedad de Tomar Pruebas

2) Hay muchas cosas que uno puede hacer para reducir o aún eliminar la ansiedad de prueba. Primero, estando bien preparado es la mejor forma de reducir esta sensación. Empieza a estudiar y revisar para tu prueba días o aún semanas antes del día para que no estés estudiando al último momento en la noche anterior. Seguidamente, ejercitando 45-60 minutos cada día ayuda a reducir la tensión general y puede mejorar tu concentración y memoria. Otras formas de reducir la tensión de prueba es dormir bien por la noche, comer un desayuno saludable con proteína, y presentarte temprano a la clase para que puedas revisar tus notas una última vez. Siguiendo estas sugerencias te ayudará a sentirte mejor preparado, pero ¿Qué puedes hacer cuando estás tomando la prueba?

Sugerencias para Probar Mejor

3) Una vez que tienes la prueba en tus manos pudieras creer que no hay nada más que hacer más que preocuparte. Sin embargo, puedes ser un probador más listo siguiendo los siguientes consejos:

*Cuidadosamente lee las direcciones 3 veces para que sepas lo que se espera que hagas. Si estás confundido por algo, preguntale a tu profesor.

*Lee toda la prueba para que sepas cuanto tiempo tienes para usar en cada problema.

*Apunta las formulas, definiciones, o datos importantes en los márgenes para que no te preocupes por olvidarlos.

*Contesta primero los problemas fáciles: esto te ayuda a sentirte más seguro.

*Antes de escribir tu respuesta, lee todas tus opciones y tacha las que sabes que son incorrectas.

*Si te sientes nervioso, vete más despacio y toma 3-4 suspiros; esto te ayudará enfocarte.

*Finalmente, revisa tus respuestas y asegúrate de que contestaste cada pregunta.

4) Tomando pruebas puede ser tenso, pero estando preparado y siguiendo estos consejos te ayudará a relajarte y a hacer lo mejor que puedes.

Name_____ Title of Text: "Test-Taking Tips"

Prediction: I predict this article is about...

PreDuringPostCornell Notes

Questions	Answers
1. **What** is test anxiety?	1.
2. **How** can I reduce this anxiety?	2.
3. **What** can I do to be a better test taker?	3.

Vocabulary

prepared-

overwhelmed-

Paragraph Shrink
Focus Words:

Water and Your Health
Julie Adams

1) There are six *nutrients* essential for a healthy body: carbohydrates, proteins, fats, vitamins, minerals and water. While many of us are aware of the importance of having a balanced diet with all of these nutrients included, many do not know just how important one of them is...water. In fact, one can only survive a few days without water but many days or even weeks without the other nutrients.

How Important is Water?

2) Our bodies consist of 75% water. Our brain, blood and lungs are all over 80% water and to function properly, they rely on water. When we are only 2% *dehydrated*, our bodies go into survival mode and try to *conserve*, or save, the little water it has. This means that every single thing our body needs to do will not be done as effectively when it is lacking water.

What Happens When We Are Dehydrated?

3) When we do not drink enough water, our entire body suffers. A dehydrated brain may make you feel dizzy, nauseous, grumpy, and/or tired. You also may not be able to solve a simple math problem or understand what you read. Water helps to regulate blood sugar and when we don't drink enough, we crave food. Our bones can also become brittle without enough water. There are many other problems a dehydrated person may have: thickening of the blood, which may lead to a stroke or heart attack, hair loss, joint pain, bad breath, constipation, or an increased risk of certain cancers.

Beverages that Zap Water

4) It may seen strange but what we choose to drink may actually *deplete*, or reduce, water from our bodies. Drinks that contain caffeine such as coffee, tea and soda, actually cause our body to lose precious water. Alcohol also robs water from the body and can lead to alcohol poisoning, which can be deadly.

How Much Do I Need?

5) Studies recommend that adolescents drink six to eight glasses of water a day or 50-70 ounces. If you are active or it is very warm, you may need to drink a little more to stay hydrated. Experts say the best way to tell if you are drinking enough water is to look at the color of your urine. Dark yellow urine means you need to drink water immediately; a properly hydrated person has urine that is nearly clear.

Agua y tu Salud
Julie Adams

1) Hay seis *nutrientes* esenciales para un cuerpo saludable: carbohidratos, proteínas, grasas, vitaminas, minerales y agua. Mientras que muchos de nosotros estamos conscientes de la importancia de tener una dieta balanceada con todos los nutrientes incluidos, muchos no sabemos que tan importante es uno de ellos...el agua. En realidad, uno puede sobrivivir solamente unos cuantos días sin agua pero varios días o aún semanas sin los otros nutrientes.

¿Que tan Importante es el Agua?

2) Nuestros cuerpos consisten de un 75% de agua. Nuestro cerebro, sangre y pulmones consisten de un 80% de ague y para funcionar adecuadamente, ellos dependen en el agua. Cuando estamos *deshidratados* solamente un 2%, nuestros cuerpos entran en un estado de supervivencia y tratan de *conservar*, o ahorrar, la poca agua que tienen. Esto quiere decir que cada cosa que nuestro cuerpo necesita hacer no podrá hacerse tan efectivamente cuando le hace falta ague.

¿Que Sucede Cuando Estamos Deshidratados?

3) Cuando no bebemos suficiente agua, todo nuestro cuerpo sufre. Un cerebro deshidratado pudiera hacerte sentir mareado, con náuseas, malhumorado y /o cansado. También no podrías resolver un problema simple de Matemáticas o entender lo que lees. El ague ayuda a regular el azúcar de la sangre y cuando no bebemos suficiente, se nos antoja la comida. Nuestros huesos también pueden hacerse quebradizos sin suficiente agua. Hay muchos otros problemas que una personal deshidratada pudiera tener: espesamiento de la sangre, lo cual pudiera conducir a una embolia o a un ataque cardiaco, pérdida del cabello, dolor de coyunturas, mal aliento, constipación, o riesgo elevado de ciertos cánceres.

Bebidas que Eliminan el Agua

4) Parecería extraño pero lo que elegimos para beber pudiera realmente *agotar*, o reducir, el agua de nuestros cuerpos. Bebidas que contienen cafeína tales como el café, el té, y las sodas, realmente causan a que nuestro cuerpo pierda agua valiosa. El alcohol puede conducir a envewnenamiento, lo cual puede ser mortal.

¿Cuanta Necesito?

5) Los estudios recomiendan que los adolecentes tomen de 6 a 8 vasos de agua al día o 50-70 onzas. Si estás activo o si está muy caliente, pudieras tener que beber un poco más para mantenerte hidratado. Los expertos dicen que la mejor forma de saber si estás tomando suficiente agua es viendo al color de tu orina. Orina amarilla oscura indica que necesitas beber agua inmediatamente; una persona propiamente hidratada tiene la orina casi clara.

Prediction: I predict this article is about...

PreDuringPostCornell Notes

Questions	Answers
1. **What** are the essential nutrients our bodies need?	1.
2. **How** important is water?	2.
3. **What** happens when we are dehydrated?	3.
4. **Which** beverages zap water?	4.
5. **How** much water do I need?	5.

Vocabulary

nutrient-

dehydrated-

conserve-

deplete-

Paragraph Shrink
Focus Words:

Adolescent Brains
Julie Adams

Are All Brains the Same?

1) Scientists have discovered some surprising differences between adolescent and adult brain development. An adolescent brain is different than an adult's because it is highly influenced by the *amygdala*, a region of the brain associated with impulse and aggression. This may explain why tweens and teens sometimes feel misunderstood and angered by others and overrreact to a situation (drama, drama, drama).

What Does Science Say?

2) Until recently, many scientists believed a brain fully developed by age twelve. However, recent studies have shown that the brain does not fully mature until a person is in his early twenties. New findings show that an adolescent brain lacks development in the *prefrontal cortex*, an area that controls decision-making, emotions and planning and organization.

If I Don't Turn My Homework In...

3) Teens may also have more difficulty understanding cause and effect. Many experts believe this lack of brain development is why the adolescent *mortality* and *morbidity* rate is 200-300% higher than any other age group. A teen is more likely to make reckless decisions regarding driving, substance abuse and participating in dangerous activities without proper protection, than an adult with a fully developed brain. Many times, a young brain does not understand the consequences of a poor decision and that can lead to trouble.

Can Anything Be Done to Expedite Brain Growth?

4) There is good news, young people can "exercise" their brains by learning to control their emotions and thinking and talking through their decisions. This helps to understand situations better before saying or doing something you may regret. Before making a decision, ask yourself, "What is the best thing that can happen if I do this? What is the worst?" If the negative outweighs the positive, don't do it.

5) Teens may also be able to control how their brains are 'hard-wired' for the future. By focusing energy and attention on playing sports, learning an instrument, reading, especially non-fiction, or doing mathematical equations, they will be better prepared for the future. Exposure to these activities may help brain connections develop at a quicker rate.

Cerebros de los Adolescentes
Julie Adams

¿Son Iguales Todos los Cerebros?

1) Los científicos han descubierto algunas diferencias sorprendentes entre el desarrollo del cerebro de los adolescentes y el de los adultos. El cerebro de un adolescente es diferente del de un adulto porque está altamente influenciado por la *amígdala*, una región del cerebro asociada con el impulso y la agresión. Esto puede explicar porque las personas entre los 11 y 19 años de edad a veces se sienten malentendidos y enojados por otros y sobre reaccionan a la situación (drama, drama, drama).

¿Qué Dice la Ciencia?

2) Hasta hace poco, muchos científicos creían que un cerebro se desarrollaba completamente por la edad de doce. Sin embargo, estudios recientes han demostrado que el cerebro no se madura totalmente hasta que una persona está en sus tempranos veintes. Nuevos descubrimientos demuestran que al cerebro de un adolescente le falta desarrollo en la *corteza pre frontal*, au área que controla la toma de decisiones, emociones y planeamiento y organización.

Si no entrego mi tarea...

3) Los adolescentes también pueden tener dificultad entendiendo causa y efecto. Muchos expertos creen que esta falta de desarrollo cerebral es el porqué el índice de *mortalidad* y de *morbosidad* es 200-300% más alto que ningún otro grupo de edad. Es más fácil que un adolescente haga decisiones imprudentes concernientes al manejo de autos, abuso de substancias y particpando en actividades peligrosas sin protección propia, que un adulto con el cerebro totalmente desarrollado. Muchas veces, un cerebro joven no entiende las consecuencias de una mala decisión y eso puede llevar a problemas.

¿Hay Algo Que se Pueda Hacer Para Acelerar el Crecimiento del Cerebro?

4) Hay buenas noticias; la gente joven puede "ejercitar" sus cerebros aprendiendo a controlar sus emociones y pensando y hablando a través de sus decisiones. Esto ayuda a mejor entender situaciones antes de decir o hacer algo de lo cual te arrepentirás. Antes de hacer una decisión, pregúntate a ti mismo, "¿Que es lo mejor que puede suceder si hago esto?" Si lo negativo sobre pesa lo positivo, no lo hagas.

5) Los adolescentes también pudieran controlar como sus cerebros están diseñados para el futuro. Enfocando energía y atención en jugar deportes, aprendiendo un instrumento, leyendo, especialmente no ficción, o haciendo ecuaciones matemáticas, ellos estarán mejor preparados para el futuro. Exposición a estas actividades puede ayudar a que las conexiones cerebrales se desarrollen a un paso más rápido.

Name_____ Title of Text: "Adolescent Brains"

Prediction: I predict this article is about...

PreDuringPostCornell Notes

Questions	Answers
1. **Are** all brains the same?	1.
2. **What** does science say?	2.
3. **Why** are teens more likely to make risky decisions?	3.
4. **Can** anything be done to help brain growth?	4.

Vocabulary

Paragraph Shrink
Focus Words:

amygdala-

prefrontal cortex-

mortality-

morbidity-

J.Adams/AEC/2010

Skin Care for Adolescents
Julie Adams

Skin Problems You Face

1) Adolescents often face more problems with their skin than any other age group. Unpredictable hormones can cause skin to be oilier or drier than usual, resulting in redness, breakouts, and other skin conditions, such as eczema. These problems are often *associated* with the extra hormones during puberty.

Food & Beverages Can Heal or Damage

2) Adolescents sometimes do not make the healthiest food and beverage choices which can *contribute* to problem skin. Drinking soda and other caffeinated products zap skin of *hydration*, or proper fluid levels, causing dryness, leading to an overproduction of oil, thus causing breakouts. Replacing soda with plenty of water provides skin with the necessary hydration to cleanse the skin and flush out *impurities*. Eating greasy potato chips and sugary items and then touching your face can also cause breakouts. On the other hand, eating fruits and vegetables provides the vitamins and minerals the skin needs to cleanse and replenish. Eating lean meats such as tuna and chicken provides protein that helps our skin rebuild after suffering damage during the day.

Recommended Skin Care Routine

3) Healthy skin needs a balanced cleansing and care routine. One should cleanse the skin both morning and night using a mild facial cleanser with an oil-absorbing product such as salicylic acid. If you wear make-up, experts recommend you wash two times, once to remove the make-up, then again to remove the dirt and oil. Use warm water to rinse the cleanser thoroughly. Follow with a light, non-greasy moisturizer containing an SPF to hydrate and protect the skin. Also, *exfoliate* weekly with an exfoliating product designed for your skin type; this gently removes dead skin and dirt build-up. Follow these tips and enjoy healthy, clear skin in no time.

Cuidado de la Piel para Adolescentes
Julie Adams

Problemas de la Piel a los que te Enfrentas

1) Los adolescentes a menudo se enfrentan a más problemas con sus pieles que ningún otro grupo de edad. Hormonas impredecibles pueden causar que la piel sea más aceitosa o más seca que lo normal, resultando en enrojecimiento, sarpullido, y otras condiciones de la piel, tales como eczema. Estos problemas a menudo están *asociados* con las hormonas extras durante la pubertad.

Las Comidas y las Bebidas Pueden Sanar o Perjudicar

2) A veces los adolescentes no hacen las mejores elecciones de comida saludable y bebidas lo cual puede *contribuir* a piel problemática. Bebiendo soda y otros productos con cafeína privan a la piel de *hidratación*, o de niveles propios de líquidos, causando sequedad, llevando a una sobreproducción de aceite, causando sarpullido. Reemplazando la soda con bustante agua provee a la piel con la hidratación necesaria para limpiar la piel y eliminar las *impurezas*. Comiendo papas fritas grasosas y cosas azucardas y después tocarte la cara también puede causar sarpullido. Por otro lado, comiendo frutas y vegetables proveen las vitaminas y minerales que tu piel necesita para limpiarse y reponerse. Comiendo carnes de poca grasa tales como el atún y el pollo proveen proteína que ayuda a nuestra piel a reconstruirse después de haber sufrido daños durante el día.

Rutina Recomendada para el Cuidado de la Piel

3) La piel saludable necesita una rutina de cuidado y limpieze balanceada. Uno debería de limpiarsse la piel en ambas, por la mañana y por la noche usando un limpiador facial ligero con un producto absorbente de aceite tal como ácido salicílico. Si usas maquillaje, los expertos recomiendan que te laves dos veces; una para remover el maquillaje, y otra para remover la mugre y el aceite. Usa agua tibia para enjuagar totalmente el limpiador. Sigue con un humectante ligero no grasoso que contenga un SPF (Factor de Protección Solar) para hidratar y proteger la piel. También, *exfóliate* semanalmente con un producto exfoliante diseñado para tu tipo de piel; esto remueve con cuidado la piel muerta y la acumulación de mugre. Sigue estas sugerencias y goza una piel saludable y clara rápidamente.

Name_____ Title of Text: "Skin Care for Adolescents"

Prediction: I predict this article is about...

PreDuringPostCornell Notes

Questions	Answers
1. **What** are skin problems that adolescents often face?	1.
2. **How** can food and beverages heal or damage the skin?	2.
3.**What** is a recommended skin care routine for healthy skin?	3.

Vocabulary

Paragraph Shrink
Focus Words:

associated-

contribute-

hydration-

impurities-

exfoliate-

J.Adams/AEC/2010

Samples
of
PDP Cornell Notes
across the
Content Areas

Name_____ Title of Text: *Animal Farm* ch. 1

Prediction: I predict this article is about_____because
_____

PreDuringPostCornell Notes

Questions	Answers
1. What is the meeting in the barn about?	1.
2. Which human habits does Major forbid?	2.
3. Which of Major's ideas is too simplistic and won't work?	3.
4. What makes Major a "major" character?	4.

Vocabulary

tyranny-
comrade-
vice-
irony-

Paragraph Shrink

Focus Words: animals, Major, dream, rebellion

Prediction: I predict this chapter is about_____

PreDuringPostCornell Notes

Questions

Answers

1. What are the operations with functions?

1.

2. What is the composite of a function?

2.

3. What is an inverse function?

3.

4. What is the property of inverse functions?

4.

Vocabulary

Domain-
Range-
Composition-
Composite-
Function-
Inverse-

Paragraph Shrink

Focus Words: function, inverse, operations, composite

Name_____ Title of Text: Chemistry as a Science

Prediction: I predict this chapter is about_____

PreDuringPostCornell Notes

Questions	Answers
1. Why is Chemistry a central science?	1.
2. What is matter?	2.
3. What are mass and weight?	3.
4. What are branches in the field of chemistry?	4.

Vocabulary	Paragraph Shrink
Chemistry- Matter- Mass- Weight- Model-	**Focus Words:** Chemistry, matter, mass, volume

Name_____ Title of Text: "Plants and Animals Together"

Prediction: I predict this article is about_____

PreDuringPostCornell Notes

Questions	Answers
1. What is a grassland?	1. A grassland is a dry place with a lot of _____.
2. Where can small animals hide in a grassland?	2. In a grassland, small animals can hide in a _____ in the ground.
3. What is a forest?	3. A forest is a place with a lot of _____.
4. How can a tree help an animal?	4. A tree can provide an animal with _____ or be its'_____.

Vocabulary

Habitat-a place an animal lives.

Grassland-a dry place with a lot of grass.

Forest-a place with many trees.

Scaffolded Paragraph Shrink

A dry, grassy habitat that animals can live in is _____ and a habitat with many trees is called a _____.

J.Adams/AEC/2010

Other Books by Julie Adams:

Teaching Academic Vocabulary Effectively, Part I
ISBN: 978-0-595-43356-8

Teaching Academic Vocabulary Effectively, Part II
ISBN: 978-0-595-46015-1

Teaching Academic Vocabulary Effectively, Part III
ISBN: 978-0-595-49966-3

Thank You

I want to thank my husband, Chris, who has been a faithful supporter and source of wisdom to me for over half my life. You are an outstanding husband, father, friend and administrator and I thank God for you every day.

My daughters, Madeline and Grace, you are so kind, intelligent and beautiful and I am blessed to have been chosen to be your "mama." You are so precious to me.

Thank you God for reminding me of the important things in life: You, family and serving others. Strengthen me to be a blessing to You.

CPSIA information can be obtained at www.ICGtesting.com
Printed in the USA
BVOW10s0138121115

426608BV00002BB/56/P